HUNGARY

Crossroads of Europe

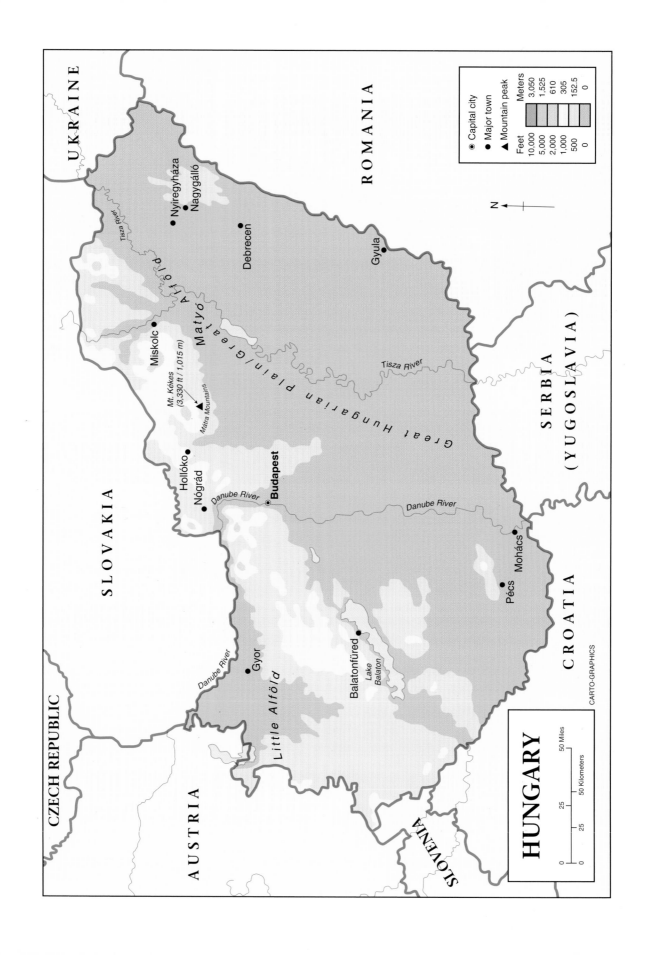

UKRAINE

ROMANIA

SERBIA
(YUGOSLAVIA)

CROATIA

SLOVENIA

AUSTRIA

SLOVAKIA

CZECH REPUBLIC

Nyiregyháza
Nagygálló
Debrecen
Gyula
Miskolc
Mt. Kékes
(3,330 ft / 1,015 m)
Mátra Mountains
Hollóko
Nógrád
Budapest
Győr
Balatonfüred
Lake Balaton
Pécs
Mohács

Tisza River
Tisza River
Danube River
Danube River
Danube River

Great Hungarian Plain/Great Alföld
Matyó
Little Alföld

N

CARTO-GRAPHICS

| Capital city |
| Major town |
| Mountain peak |

Feet	Meters
10,000	3,050
5,000	1,525
2,000	610
1,000	305
500	152.5
0	0

HUNGARY

0   25   50 Miles
0   25   50 Kilometers

EXPLORING CULTURES OF THE WORLD

HUNGARY

Crossroads of Europe

Richard Steins

BENCHMARK BOOKS

MARSHALL CAVENDISH
NEW YORK

With thanks to the Hungarian Embassy in Washington, D.C., for assistance and information, and to Csilla Strbik, who writes for Hungarian magazines, for her expert review of the manuscript.

Benchmark Books
Marshall Cavendish Corporation
99 White Plains Road
Tarrytown, New York 10591-9001

Library of Congress Cataloging-in-Publication Data
Steins, Richard.
    Hungary: Crossroads of Europe / by Richard Steins.
       p.   cm. — (Exploring cultures of the world)
    Includes bibliographical references and index.
    Summary: Describes the geography, history, culture, and people of Hungary.
    ISBN 0-7614-0141-5
    1. Hungary—Juvenile literature. [1. Hungary.] I. Title. II. Series.
DB906.S74   1997
943.9—dc21
96-51582
CIP
AC

Printed in Hong Kong

Series design by Carol Matsuyama

Front cover: Woman and child in traditional dress
Back cover: The Fishermen's Bastion in Budapest

Photo Credits
Front cover, back cover and page 36: ©Steve Vidler/Leo de Wys; title page and pages 28–29: ©Miwako Ikeda/International Stock Photo; page 6: Winfield I. Parks, Jr./National Geographic Image Collection; pages 9, 25, 50: James L. Stanfield/National Geographic Image Collection; pages 12, 13, 56: North Wind Picture Archives; pages 15, 18: AP/Wide World Photos Inc.; pages 20, 30, 38: Chad Ehlers/International Stock Photo; page 23: Bruce Dale/National Geographic Image Collection; page 26: Hubertus Kanus/Photo Researchers, Inc.; page 32: Marka/International Stock Photo; page 34: ©Robin Laurance/Photo Researchers, Inc.; page 37: ©Fred Lyon/Photo Researchers, Inc.; pages 40, 52: Thomas Nebbia/National Geographic Image Collection; page 43: ©Geiersperger/Explorer/Photo Researchers, Inc.; page 45: ©Lipnitzki/Explorer/Photo Researchers, Inc.; page 47: ©Oldrich Karasek/Peter Arnold, Inc.; pages 48, 53: ©Porterfield/Chickering/Photo Researchers, Inc.; page 49: ©Perigot/Explorer/Photo Researchers, Inc.; page 55: ©Leo de Wys Inc./De Wys/TPL/Masnikosa; page 57: ©Giulio Veggi/White Star/Photo Researchers Inc.

Contents

Map of Hungary ....Frontispiece

1 GEOGRAPHY AND HISTORY
The Fertile Crossroads 7

2 THE PEOPLE
Hungarians at Home and Abroad 21

3 FAMILY LIFE, FESTIVALS, AND FOOD
The Hungarian Way 33

4 SCHOOL AND RECREATION
Strict Schools, Easy Spas 41

5 THE ARTS
Treasures Old and New 51

Country Facts 60

Glossary 62

For Further Reading 62

Index 63

Historic Budapest, on the banks of the Danube River, reminds modern-day Hungarians of their long history and the nation's legendary founder, Prince Árpád.

1
HISTORY AND GEOGRAPHY

The Fertile Crossroads

Prince Árpád and the 1,000-Mile Walk

A long time ago, seven tribes of people lived on a broad, flat stretch of land in eastern Europe. Each tribe had a chief. The tribes were related and spoke the same language. The people were called Magyars.

The Magyars were nomadic. They moved from one place to another in search of pasture for their sheep and goats. In the late A.D. 800s, they were offered a chance to settle down in one place. Emperor Arnulf, whose kingdom was in western Europe, asked the Magyars to help him conquer an enemy. In return, he offered them land.

An advance party of Magyars traveled west to scout out the land to see if it was worth accepting Arnulf's offer. They reported back that the faraway land was flat and fertile and that not many people lived there. It was a good place to move to, they thought.

The Magyars chose one of their seven chiefs to be the leader of all the tribes. He was Prince Árpád, the head of the strongest and largest Magyar tribe.

Prince Árpád led his people on a long and arduous journey. They walked 1,000 miles (1,600 kilometers) to their new home in the west.

Through blistering summer heat and bitter winter cold, the entire Magyar people—all seven tribes—trudged across vast plains and struggled over treacherous mountains. When they arrived in the land that is now eastern Hungary, they settled down. And there the nation of Hungary had its start.

Not much more is known about Prince Árpád, because written records were not kept among the early Magyars. But the legendary leader is considered the founder of Hungary. Today, Árpád is celebrated in story and song for his courage and fearlessness. His long, fateful journey from the east to the west created a nation unlike any other.

Land of the Danube

Hungary is located in central Europe. It is bordered by seven small nations: Slovakia, Ukraine, Romania, Serbia, Croatia, Slovenia, and Austria.

The broad Danube River divides Hungary down the middle. To the east of the river lies a vast flat area called the Great Hungarian Plain, or the Great Alföld. To the west are the regions of Transdanubia and the Little Alföld. Western Hungary has some hilly areas, as does the northern part of the country, where the Mátra Mountains border on Slovakia. But Hungary is mainly flat. Its highest point, Mount Kékes, is only 3,330 feet (1,015 meters) above sea level.

Hungary's Lake Balaton is the largest freshwater lake in central Europe. Extending 45 miles (72 kilometers) in length, Balaton is shallow, perfect for boating, fishing, and swimming.

Hungary has a temperate climate. In the winter, temperatures may fall below freezing, and there is much snow and dampness. In the summer, though, the weather turns warm. It is a good time to enjoy the waters of Lake Balaton.

Broad fertile plains like this one attracted the Magyar tribes.

When the Land Was Called Pannonia

Hungary, because of its central location, has always been a crossroads—a place where people met, and usually clashed. For centuries, invaders and warring armies have crisscrossed the land, often bringing with them misery and ruin.

The ancient Romans arrived in the area west of the Danube in 35 B.C. It was not long before they had conquered what is now western Hungary. They named the land Pannonia. The people living there, who were descendants of an ancient group known as the Celts, did not submit easily to Roman rule. They resented Rome's heavy taxation. They were also angry that their young men were forced to serve in the Roman army. Over the years, several rebellions broke out against Roman authority. The Romans were eventually forced to build forts to protect themselves, and they were not able to extend their empire into what is now eastern Hungary.

By the late A.D. 300s, Pannonia was under attack by the Huns, a much-feared Germanic tribe. The Romans had finally had enough; they decided to withdraw.

The Huns then occupied the region, but they were soon replaced by other people, who in turn were pushed out by others. No one group seemed capable of holding on to the land.

The Arrival of the Magyars

The region was finally invaded by a people who would stay—the Magyars. Modern Hungarians are direct descendants of the Magyars, the people Prince Árpád led about 1,100 years ago.

After they had settled down, the Magyars were eager to expand their territory. They launched fierce attacks into lands as far away as Italy and Germany.

In A.D. 955, the Magyars were defeated at a decisive battle in Germany. As a result, they gave up hopes of further conquest. They contented themselves instead with the land that is now Hungary.

The inhabitants of western Europe were terrified of the Magyars, because they thought they were related to the dreaded Huns. They were wrong. As a result of this association, however, the Magyars acquired a new name: the Hungarians.

Prince Árpád's descendants ruled the Hungarians for the next 300 years. During this time—in the late 900s—the people accepted the Christian religion. In the year 1000, King Stephen was crowned as the first Christian king of Hungary.

Hungary's Foreign Rulers

Over the years, numerous European nobles married members of the Árpád Dynasty. (A dynasty is a line of rulers in one family.) As a result, many European leaders had the right to claim the Hungarian crown. In the early 1300s, it passed to a Frenchman—Charles Robert of Anjou. He was called King Charles I.

Thus began a long period in which Hungarian kings were foreign-born. Many of these rulers were interested in expanding Hungarian territory. Charles's son, Louis I, conquered much of the surrounding region. During his reign, the boundaries of Hungary extended far beyond those of the present day.

The Turkish Conquest

By the early 1500s, Hungary faced a powerful threat from the Turkish people in the east. The Turks were expanding their empire. Gradually they were moving into western Europe, conquering everyone in their path. In 1526, they defeated the Hungarian army at the Battle of Mohács, in southern Hungary.

The Turkish conquest had a devastating effect on the nation, which broke apart for a while. The Turks occupied the central area of Hungary, including the capital city of Budapest. The eastern province of Transylvania remained under the control of the Hungarians. The far western part of Hungary came under the control of Austria, its neighbor.

After the Battle of Mohács, the Muslim Turks continued to fight the Christian Hungarians in the eastern part of the country. Here, Turks lay siege to a Hungarian town.

Many Hungarians in central Hungary fled from the Turks. Large parts of the country resembled ghost towns. The people feared having to live under the rule of the "Infidels." The Turks were Muslims, followers of the religion of Islam. Christianity and Islam had long been at odds.

The Rule of the Hapsburgs

After they had defeated the Hungarians, the Turks continued to threaten western Europe. By 1683, they were at the gates of Vienna, the capital of Austria. There they were stopped. That defeat was a blow to Turkish rule in Europe. Eventually, the Turks retreated from Hungary. In their place came the Austrians, who took control of the entire country. In 1687,

Leopold, the Hapsburg ruler of Austria, became the king of Hungary.

The rule of the Hapsburgs brought a period of peace and prosperity to Hungary, especially under Empress Maria Theresa. She reigned for a long time—from 1740 until 1780. Many Hungarians, however, wanted to be free of foreign rule. In 1848, they tried to push the Austrians out but were not successful.

Empress Maria Theresa. The long-reigning Hapsburg monarch brought many years of peace and prosperity to Hungary.

The Austrians decided to give the Hungarians more of a say in their affairs. In 1867, they created a "dual monarchy," called Austria-Hungary. Under this arrangement, the Austrian emperor would also be crowned king of Hungary. However, Hungarians would have more control over their day-to-day lives.

The End of an Empire

The empire of Austria-Hungary lasted for 51 years. It was destroyed in 1918, at the end of World War I. Austria-Hungary and Germany were defeated by the Allies, a group of countries led by the United States and Great Britain.

The terms of the peace plan imposed on Austria-Hungary by the Allies after the war were severe. Under this plan, Hungary was separated from Austria, and more than two thirds of its territory was given to surrounding countries. Thus, millions of Hungarians suddenly found themselves separated from their native land and living in several neighboring countries.

The new, shrunken Hungary was a small and weak state. In the years after World War I, it experienced many political and economic problems.

World War II

When World War II broke out in Europe in 1939, Hungarian leaders hoped to remain neutral. They hoped to stay out of the war by not taking sides in it. Once again, however, Hungary's central location in Europe made it a crossroads of conflict. In 1941, realizing that neutrality was impossible, the leaders of Hungary decided to join the side of Nazi Germany. It was a fatal error.

Hungary paid a bitter price for its alliance with Germany. Much of the beautiful old capital city of Budapest was destroyed, and thousands of Hungarians lost their lives.

The Royal Palace in Budapest was nearly destroyed by bombs in World War II. It has since been carefully restored.

A Communist Dictatorship

In the last year of the war, just before Nazi Germany was defeated, Hungary was invaded by the Soviet Union. The troops of this Communist state remained after the war ended in 1945. By 1948, Hungary was completely under Communist control.

Under communism, Hungarians could no longer own their own businesses or land—everything belonged to the state. They also had no say in the government. Anyone who criticized the government met with swift punishment. Some were even killed.

All hopes for democratic government—rule by the people and their elected representatives—were crushed. Hungary became a "satellite" state of the Soviet Union. Like the moon is a satellite of the earth, Hungary was in the grip of the Soviet Union. The people were forced to follow all of the political, social, and economic policies of the Russians.

The years after the war were difficult ones for Hungarians. There were shortages of housing and food. In 1953, Imre Nagy, a moderate Communist, came to power in Hungary. The Soviets were not happy with Nagy. They wanted a tougher Communist leader in Hungary. In 1955, the Soviets replaced him with one of their "puppets"—someone who would do exactly what they wanted. The Hungarian people, however, were ready to demand their freedom.

1956: Year of Revolution

In October 1956, a full-scale revolt against the Communists broke out in Hungary. Ordinary citizens took up arms in the streets of Budapest and the surrounding countryside to protest against the government. The uprising was bloody.

Stunned citizens look on as a Soviet tank enters Budapest. It took only a few days for the Soviets to crush the 1956 Hungarian Revolution.

During the height of the fighting, Nagy, who was popular with the people, was returned to power.

But the Soviets would not allow such a rebellion. Within days, Soviet troops and tanks entered Hungary and brutally crushed the revolution. Thousands of Hungarians were killed, and more than 200,000 fled into Austria to escape arrest and execution. (Many later settled in the United States and

HUNGARIAN GOVERNMENT

Hungary is a parliamentary democracy. The people run their country through their elected representatives in Parliament. The head of government is the prime minister, who is the leader of the party that has the most votes in Parliament. As head of government, the prime minister runs the day-to-day affairs of the government, assisted by appointed ministers. The head of state is the president, who is elected by members of the Parliament. This role is not as important as the prime ministership.

The Parliament makes the nation's laws. It has 386 members. Of these, 176 are elected directly by the voters. Members of certain political parties receive the other seats. Like the prime minister and president, members of Parliament serve four-year terms.

At the top of the Hungarian judicial system is the Supreme Court. Courts also exist at the local level.

other countries.) Imre Nagy was arrested and jailed. Two years later, he was executed by the government after a secret trial.

The Soviets then made János Kádár the head of Hungary. He believed that, one day, many good changes would be possible if Hungary did not challenge the Soviet Union's authority.

The Long Road to Reform

In the late 1960s, Kádár cautiously began to make some changes, or reforms. He allowed limited private ownership of property. Some Hungarian farmers were allowed to grow crops for private sale. And some businesses were allowed to operate for private profit.

Gradually, living conditions in Hungary improved. There were more goods for people to buy and more money for people to spend. Many Hungarians soon began to push for greater freedoms, including the right to form political parties. But it wasn't until 1989 that Hungarians were finally free to run their own economy and government.

Free At Last

In 1989, the Soviet empire began to crumble. In the following year, Hungarians voted in their first free election. A non-Communist became the prime minister, or head of the government. The Hungarian Communist Party, which had changed its name to the Socialist Party, was just another political party competing for votes.

The new government soon began to return many industries to private ownership. By 1993, more than half of Hungarian industry was privately owned.

This change from a government-controlled economy to a capitalist system, or free-market economy, created new problems for the Hungarians. For the first time since the end of World War II, there was unemployment. The old Communist system had provided people with job security, retirement pensions, and health care. Now the average person had to take more responsibility for his or her life. People were frightened about the future.

Because of these problems, in 1994, the former Communists won the parliamentary elections and a former Communist became the prime minister. The country did not return to the old days, however. Hungary's leaders remain committed to the capitalist system. And there are numerous political parties, which are free to make changes in the future.

Dressed in traditional clothes, a Hungarian Gypsy strums the zither.

2
THE PEOPLE

Hungarians at Home and Abroad

Compared to many other nations, Hungary does not have many people. Its entire population is only a little over 10 million—just half the number of people who live in the city of Cairo, Egypt!

About 90 percent of the people are ethnic Hungarians—they are descendants of the Magyars. The remainder of the population consists of Gypsies; people of Germanic background; and small numbers of Romanians, Serbs, Slovaks, and Croats.

Today, about 30 percent of all Hungarians in the world live outside of Hungary. Many live in the countries that border on Hungary, such as Romania, Slovakia, and Croatia. Areas of these countries were once part of the larger Austria-Hungarian territory. Many Hungarians also live in Australia, western Europe, Canada, and the United States.

Hungary's Biggest Minority

In 1902, the Austrian Archduke Joseph wrote the following:

Who has not seen . . . those wandering hordes, traveling from village to village in their covered wagons drawn by wretched nags? Who does not know of the dark strangers who live out their wretched lives in mud huts on the fringes of our villages? Whose heart has not been overcome by deep emotion on hearing these "new Magyar" musicians strike up their wailing melodies?

The "strangers" Joseph was writing about were the Gypsies of Hungary, who are the largest ethnic minority in the country today. "Hungarians" and "Gypsies" have often been confused. They are sometimes thought to be the same people. Actually, the Gypsies are an ancient nomadic people who came to Europe from Asia a long time ago. They call themselves the "Roma," and they live in other countries besides Hungary.

Traveling from village to village in Hungary, the Gypsies were often horse traders, door-to-door salesmen, and beggars. Many of the Gypsies were also musicians. On their violins they played the sad melodies that are a familiar part of Hungarian music.

Gypsies have always lived apart. They have their own social rules and traditions, and they usually do not mix with other people. As a result, they have often been the object of prejudice, suspicion, and even violence. During World War II, the Nazis rounded up Gypsies throughout much of Europe and sent them to be killed in concentration camps. The Gypsies were nearly wiped out.

A Gypsy woman and her child. Gypsies have lived for centuries in Hungary, but always on the fringes of society.

Today, Hungarian Gypsies do not usually travel in wagons. They are, however, among the poorest people in Hungary. And they still live apart, in communities on the fringes of large cities. Many of them are poorly paid unskilled workers and day laborers.

The Hungarian government has tried to help the Gypsies by providing education and encouraging them to become more "Hungarian." But much prejudice still exists, and the Gypsies themselves are reluctant to change. They don't want to give up their language, their age-old customs, and their sense of community.

Religion in Hungary

For centuries, Christianity has played an important role in the lives of the Hungarian people. Today, two thirds of the people are Roman Catholics. Protestants form the next-largest group. Most of these are Calvinists, and they live in the northeastern part of the country. Another Protestant group is the Lutherans. There are also smaller numbers of people who belong to the Eastern Orthodox Church.

The Jewish population of Hungary was once quite large, but it is very small today. More than 550,000 Hungarian Jews were killed by the Nazis in the 1940s, during World War II.

The practice of religion in Hungary was made very difficult once the Communists came to power in the late 1940s. The Communists did not want the Hungarians to have religious beliefs. Instead, they demanded the people's full loyalty to the Communist Party and the state. Some religious leaders were even imprisoned. Under the Communists, the government regulated the churches. Today, the government is still very involved in religious affairs.

Bountiful Farms

Even though almost half of all Hungarians live in the countryside, only one in five people works on a farm. Yet agriculture is a big industry. Hungarians grow almost all

This Hungarian farmer is gathering squash to take to market.

the food they need. They have enough left over to sell to other countries.

The major Hungarian crops are corn and wheat. Some barley, rye, and oats are also grown. Sugar beets are a very

At harvest time, a wine grower gathers grapes for pressing.

important crop, as are onions and peppers for making paprika. Paprika is a spice made of ground red peppers. It is widely used in Hungarian cooking. Hungary, in fact, produces so much paprika that it is one of the country's most important exports.

Fruits such as apricots, pears, cherries, apples, and plums are plentiful. Hungarians grow grapes and produce wine as well. Much of the wine is sold to western Europe and the United States.

Budapest, Heart of Hungary

The largest city by far in Hungary is its capital, Budapest. It is home to 20 percent of the nation's population. No other Hungarian city approaches Budapest in terms of size, appearance, or importance.

The pace of life is fast in Budapest. The streets are jammed with pedestrians and honking traffic. Many people wear fashionable and stylish clothes. Kids, like youngsters in most countries, are happy to wear jeans and sneakers.

Budapest has a mixture of old and new buildings. Many of its historic structures—churches, museums, and the homes of the nobility—were built in the late 1800s, when Hungary was ruled by the Austrians. These ornate buildings often remind visitors of the Austrian capital, Vienna. Newer buildings, constructed under the Communists, have a drab, uniform look.

These contrasts between the old and the new can also be found in Hungary's other, smaller cities. Miskolc is an industrial city in the northeastern part of the country. Debrecen, in eastern Hungary, is a university town. Pécs lies in the south, in the coal-mining region.

The beautiful Matthias Church in Budapest attracts admiring visitors from all over the world.

An Ancient Language

The Hungarian language, which is also known as Magyar, is very different from the languages spoken in western Europe. Although it has the same alphabet as English, Hungarian uses accent marks on the letters to show how words are pronounced.

Budapest is a lively city. Here on Vaci Street, shoppers admire the stores and enjoy strolling in the traffic-free road.

SAY IT IN HUNGARIAN

Here are some important words and phrases to know in Hungarian:

Hello. (Good day.)	*Jó napot.* (jo NAH-pot)
Goodbye.	*Viszontlátásra.* (vee-son-LAH-tash-rah)
How are you?	*Hogy van?* (HOD-yeh von)
I'm fine.	*Jól.* (yawl)
Yes.	*Igen.* (EE-gun)
Please.	*Kérem szépen.* (KAY-rem SAY-pen)
Thank you.	*Köszönöm.* (HOR-in)
The check, please.	*Kérem szépen a szamlat.* (KAY-rem SAY-pen uh SAHM-laht)

Egy (EG-yeh), *kettö* (KET-tuh), *három* (HA-rom), *négy* (NEG-yeh), *öt* (euht), *hat* (hot), *hét* (hayt), *nyolc* (NYO-etz), *kilenc* (KEE-lantz), *tíz* (teez): one, two, three, four, five, six, seven, eight, nine, ten.

Hungarian words are often very long. For example, the word *Goodbye* is *Viszontlátásra* in Hungarian.

Another feature of the Hungarian language is that there are no separate terms for "he" and "she." As a result, Hungarians who learn English often confuse "he" and "she," saying one when they mean the other.

Hungarians are proud of their language, which is spoken throughout the country. Tourists in large cities will find, though, that many Hungarians also speak German. In addition, more and more Hungarians are learning to speak English.

Hungarians love to go out with their friends and family. Here, musicians entertain diners at a popular Budapest restaurant.

3

FAMILY LIFE, FESTIVALS, AND FOOD

The Hungarian Way

Families are closely knit in Hungary. Most people live in nuclear families—a father, mother, and children. However, people are also close to members of their extended family: grandparents, aunts, uncles, and cousins. All of these people usually get together to celebrate the holidays, either over a hearty meal at home or in a nearby restaurant.

Hungary, like other former Communist countries in the region, suffers from a shortage of housing. A typical family of four—a father, mother, brother, and sister—in a large city often live in a cramped two-room apartment. Children might sleep on a sofa in the living room. Families are constantly in search of larger apartments, but there are few to go around. People often have to wait for years before they can find one.

Older buildings in cities like Budapest have large, old-fashioned apartments that are highly desirable, especially for growing families. Unfortunately, there are not enough of these. The newer buildings, built after World War II, are not as spacious or as well constructed. But these are in demand as well.

Several generations of this Hungarian family work together to raise animals and grow crops on their farm.

The Roles of Men and Women

Men and women have equal rights under Hungarian law. There is a long tradition of Hungarian women working outside the home. However, Hungarian men usually hold more powerful positions at work, and they are almost always paid more money than women. For example, most schoolteachers in Hungary are women, but most of their supervisors are men.

In the home, the wife is expected to cook meals and clean the house, in addition to taking care of the children, even if she holds one or more jobs. Hungarian men do not have a tradition of helping with home responsibilities, and they are used to being waited on.

The old attitudes toward women are changing slowly in Hungary, as young people are learning and thinking more about women's rights.

Holidays in Hungary

Hungarians enjoy taking part in several religious and national holidays. Since most Hungarians are Christians, they observe the main Christian holidays of Christmas (celebrated on December 25 and 26) and Easter (in the spring). The most important national holidays are the feast of St. Stephen, in honor of the first Christian king; the anniversary of the uprising against the Austrians in 1848; and the anniversary of the start of the 1956 Revolution. Hungarians of all ages enjoy marking the new year on January 1.

Hungarians celebrate their holidays much as people do in Canada and the United States. They have the day off from school and work, and they gather with family and close friends in the home or in restaurants.

Folk Festivals

Hungarians are proud of their history and traditions. They like to remember them by holding celebrations of music and dance called folk festivals. People often wear traditional clothes, such as colorfully embroidered skirts, blouses, and headdresses.

These dolls, like the couple, are dressed in bright traditional Hungarian clothes.

Festivals give these girls the chance to perform folk dances for their friends and families.

One of the largest festivals in central Europe takes place in the summer in the city of Miskolc, in northeastern Hungary. It is called the Kaláka Folklore Festival. People gather to enjoy traditional songs, storytelling, and lively dances. The festival is great fun for the entire family.

Every June thousands of people gather in Nagygálló, a town in northeastern Hungary. Visitors to the festival stay in tents and campsites in the surrounding forest. The center of the activities is a huge wooden barn, which is used for dancing. Around it, craftspeople set up their booths, where they sell beautiful handmade products, such as pottery and embroidered clothes and linens.

Mealtime

Hungarians eat their main meal at midday, whether they are at home or in the factory, office, or school. On holidays and Sundays, a family might relax and enjoy this meal in a restaurant. Eating out is very popular in Hungary, and restaurants stay open until late in the evening.

Bright red peppers, lots of nuts, gourds, and fresh garlic are displayed in a Hungarian market. The red peppers are used to make the most famous Hungarian spice: paprika.

LIPTOI CHEESE SPREAD

1 8-oz. package soft cream cheese   1 tablespoon paprika
1/4 cup soft butter   1 teaspoon dry mustard
1 teaspoon salt   1 1/2 tablespoons caraway seeds

Blend the cheese and butter in a mixing bowl. Add the remaining ingredients, mixing them well. Put the mixture into a small serving bowl. Chill in the refrigerator for at least 30 minutes. Serve on crackers or pumpernickel bread. Serves 4 to 6.

The typical Hungarian meal begins with soup. Meat and fish are usually served next, with potatoes or rice and a salad on the side. Hungarians eat a lot of chicken and pork. Freshwater fish like carp, pike, and trout, which are caught in Hungary's rivers and lakes, are also enjoyed throughout the country.

Goulash is probably the most famous Hungarian dish. It is a stew made of cubes of beef and three or four different kinds of vegetables.

Paprika is a spice that gives much Hungarian food its special flavor. It is usually made of finely ground red peppers, but sometimes green or yellow peppers are used. It can be mild or hot, depending on the cook's preference.

Hungarian desserts are world famous. Delicious pastries and cakes are often enjoyed with coffee in shops called cafés. These are popular places where Hungarians gather to relax and chat.

These young schoolchildren are enjoying lunch in their classroom.

4
SCHOOL AND RECREATION

Strict Schools,
Easy Spas

Hungarians believe that education is very important, and students take their studies seriously. All children between the ages of six and fifteen are required to go to school. The school day begins at 8:00 in the morning and usually ends at 1:00 or 2:00 in the afternoon.

Hungarian primary education is very strict and formal. Schools pay special attention to mathematics, science, and grammar. Students wear uniforms and are expected to sit quietly, listen carefully to their teachers, and speak only when given permission. In order to be promoted to the next grade, students are required to pass tests that show they are familiar with all the subjects they have studied in that grade.

Sports are considered a valuable part of education as well. Boys are usually interested in soccer. They may play on school teams or just with friends after school. Girls tend to prefer swimming, running, or tennis. Older girls often play on school teams.

Hungarian schools devote special attention to music. Students learn about their nation's rich musical heritage. They also develop skills in playing a variety of musical instruments. They learn how to develop their singing skills by using a method created by a famous Hungarian composer, Zoltán Kodály.

Hungary is also well known for special education. The Pető Institute in Budapest teaches children with cerebral palsy to walk.

Religious organizations are permitted to run their own schools in Hungary. Such private schools, however, charge fees, while state-run education is free.

After eight years of primary school, students go on to either four years of high school or two or three years of vocational school. The Hungarian high school system is similar to that of most European countries. High schools—called "gymnasiums" (the term doesn't mean physical education)—offer a general academic education. Vocational schools offer students job training in industry, business, or agriculture.

To graduate from a vocational school, students must show skill in their chosen occupations. To graduate from a gymnasium, students must pass an examination in mathematics, the Hungarian language, and history.

Those who want to attend college must also work hard to pass an entrance exam. University education usually lasts five years in Hungary.

A Love of Museums

Hungarians think of museums and historical sites as part of their ongoing education. There are many famous museums for people to visit. The Castle Hill section of Budapest, where the

One of Budapest's famous museums, the Hungarian National Gallery, holds works of fine art.

historic Royal Palace is located, is home to several museums. There visitors can choose from the Museum of Recent History; the Hungarian National Gallery, which is a showplace of Hungarian art; the Budapest Historic Museum; and the National Library.

It was at Castle Hill that Hungary's final battle of World War II took place. The beautiful old buildings were reduced to rubble. After the war, Castle Hill was painstakingly rebuilt. Old manuscripts, or handwritten books, were used to guide the reconstruction.

Outside the capital city, in other towns and cities, there are many more interesting museums. Some of these local museums contain exhibits from early Hungarian history. The Hermann Ottó Museum in Miskolc, for example, focuses on local and regional history. In Gyula, the Erkel Ferenc Museum has an extensive archaeological collection of ancient items found in the region.

Spa Traditions

Hungary's land is like a sponge: It absorbs moisture. No matter where you dig, you'll soon find water—and most of it is bubbly, hot spring water. Because of this abundance of hot springs, hundreds of spas, or health resorts, have been built across the country. Hungarians love to "take the waters," or soak in them.

Public baths are a favorite part of the spas. They were introduced long ago by the ancient Romans. It was the Turks, though, who built public bathhouses throughout the land and made them popular. The Turks' beautiful copper-domed bathhouses can still be seen in such cities as Budapest, where they are still in use. For hundred of years, Hungarians have enjoyed meeting friends at the baths and relaxing in the soothing hot waters.

Hungarians believe that the minerals in the hot spring waters cure many kinds of illness. Different spas are devoted to the healing of different ailments. The spa at Györ, for

Tall columns and potted plants adorn the pool at an elegant spa in Budapest.

Men and women "take the waters" separately by the day or hour at public baths. For example, men's bathing hours might be at 1:00 and 3:00 in the afternoon, while women use the pools at 2:00 and 4:00 P.M.

The visitor to a spa will probably start by sitting for a few minutes in a steam room. There, the temperature may go as high as 149 degrees Fahrenheit (55 degrees Centigrade). The hot steam invigorates and cleanses the skin. The steam room is then followed by a jump into a cool pool and then a splash in a heated pool. In the Turkish baths, a favorite meeting place is the heated pool under the great dome. There, sunlight streams through the colored glass of the copper dome.

example, is noted for the treatment of rheumatism and stomach problems. People with high blood pressure or heart disease often travel to the baths at Balantonfüred. The spa at Nyiregyháza is the favorite resort for those who suffer from skin problems.

Near the city of Miskolc, there is a spa that features mineral springs inside a cave. People suffering from asthma enter the dark and steamy cave in order to inhale the moist air, which seems to help their breathing problems.

A gigantic, open-air, hot spring pool in Budapest attracts people at all times of the year, even on the coldest days of winter. The fearless bathers skip through the snow between the changing rooms and the hot pool.

Sailing and Fishing

The Hungarians' love for water extends to sailing and fishing. Hungary's Lake Balaton is a magnet for Hungarian and foreign vacationers alike. After Budapest, it is the country's biggest tourist attraction.

Hungarians call the lake the "sea of Hungary." It is shallow, with an average depth of only 12 feet (3.5 meters). As a result, the water is warmed very quickly by the sun and is ideal for swimming during the summer months. The southern shore of Lake Balaton is especially shallow, which makes it a safe place for children to swim.

Sailboats have a long tradition on Balaton, going back to the 1800s. Private motorboats are not allowed on the lake. Commercial motorboats are permitted, however. People may travel across Lake Balaton on steamers that leave from a number of lakeside villages.

Lake Balaton, the largest freshwater lake in central Europe, is a favorite place to swim, sail, and fish.

A favorite pastime at the lake—and in Hungary in general—is fishing. Hungarians love to fish for the pike (called *fogas*) that fill the lake. Children and adults sit patiently at the lakeside, waiting to catch a fish. If the fish fail to bite, Hungarians will often joke that the only *fogas* they have is at home in the closet. That is because *fogas* is also the Hungarian word for "coathanger"!

A Love of Sports

Horseback riding has always been a favorite sport in Hungary, but in recent years, a number of new sporting activities have become popular. Golf can now be found at most resorts.

Horsemanship is greatly admired in Hungary. This man is performing tricks in a show.

Hungarians ice-skate beneath the towers of an old castle in Budapest.

Since golf tends to be an expensive sport, most Hungarians simply rent equipment for the day when they play.

But, like most Europeans, Hungarians have a passionate interest in soccer, which they call football. The increasing presence of television sets in Hungarian homes has made these fans very happy. They often watch soccer as well as many other European and international sporting events.

A guitarist and flutist play centuries-old music in a quiet spot in Budapest's historic district.

5

THE ARTS

Treasures Old and New

For hundreds of years, ordinary people have been producing beautiful works of art in Hungary. Hungarian craftspeople are famous for their delicate embroidery, beautiful pottery, and hand-carved wood products. Besides these folk crafts, Hungary is noted for the important contributions its artists have made in the fields of music and writing.

Preserving the Old Ways

The Hungarians have had to struggle to keep their ancient traditions. During the long rule of the Turks, the Hungarian language and crafts were seen as a threat to Turkish power. After World War I, Hungarians lost two thirds of their land to neighboring countries. Some of the old ways of doing things were lost as well because so many people were forced to live in different countries.

At a small street market, shoppers examine dolls dressed in colorful costumes.

Today, however, visitors to Hungary can find folk art for sale almost everywhere in the country. The Matyó region east of Budapest, for example, is famous as a textile and crafts center. Some of the most colorful folk costumes can be found for sale in shops throughout the area. On holidays, people often wear traditional Hungarian clothing. These include brightly colored shirts and blouses and intricately patterned full skirts. Another typical Hungarian folk costume is the long, fleecy coat worn by shepherds. The coat extends from the shoulders to the ground.

Hungarians are noted for their pottery. The most familiar Hungarian pottery features traditional flower patterns that are also seen in embroidery on skirts and blouses. A unique kind of pottery dates back to the period of Turkish rule. These pots are baked in a kiln, or oven, that uses black coal. A dark gray or black background forms on the clay, on which the potter carves patterns with a pebble.

Outdoor markets have a long history in Hungary. Today, they usually feature a mix of folk crafts and manufactured products. As in the past, people go to the markets not only to buy things but also to visit with their neighbors and friends.

Most towns have a market that attracts people in search of bargains. One of the most famous markets is found in the city of Pécs, in southern Hungary. It is held on the first Sunday of every month. If the weather is good, huge crowds jam the marketplace, which is near the city's main railroad station. Shoppers can find everything there from birds and cats to clothing, flowers, food, and local arts and crafts.

Traditional Architecture

In some rural areas of Hungary, traditional folk architecture has been carefully preserved. The region of Nógrád, for example, north of Budapest, is noted for its beautiful timber

Two friends from the historic village of Hollókö wear traditional folk dress.

farmhouses. In the village of Hollókö there are fifty-five historic houses. Built in the old Hungarian style, they are adorned with intricately carved wood. Today they are home mainly to older women, who dress in traditional clothing. One of the houses has been converted into a museum of farm utensils, while several others serve as small hotels for visiting travelers.

A Love of Music

There are two kinds of Hungarian music. One is folk music, which often contains Gypsy sounds. The other is classical music. It is more complex and formal than folk music, though it often includes folk melodies and rhythms.

Songs of the People

Hungarian folk music is centuries old. It was rarely written down, however. Instead, it was played in the villages and was passed down from generation to generation. Hungarian folk songs use a five-note scale, which is different from the European seven-note scale. The folk songs were often accompanied by a shepherd's flute, which was made of elderberry. Another peasant instrument was the bagpipe, which was in wide use into the 1800s.

Perhaps the most famous instrument associated with Hungarian folk music is the zither. It is a many-stringed instrument that is played with a pick and one's fingers. Along with the violin, the *cymbalom* is often played by the Gypsies. It is a trapeze-shaped, stringed instrument with bent-up ends that is played with two wooden sticks. Today, Gypsy bands that play in Hungarian restaurants often use a metal variation of the *cymbalom*.

A musician plays a lively folk song on the accordion, a popular instrument in Hungary.

Almost every town and village now has its own folk music and dance groups. They often play at the local folk festivals that are held across the nation.

Classical Sounds

Perhaps the most famous Hungarian composer of classical music is Franz Liszt. He lived in the 1800s and is known especially for the music he composed for the piano. He was a great pianist. Although Liszt lived much of his life outside of Hungary, he helped establish a classical music tradition in his homeland. He trained a generation of pianists and teachers and left a lasting impact on musical life in Hungary.

In the music of the 1900s, the name of two Hungarians stand out: Béla Bartók and Zoltán Kodály. These world-famous composers are both known for using Hungarian folk melodies in their classical compositions. As a young composer, Bartók traveled from village to village throughout Hungary. He interviewed the people and recorded the folk songs they remembered. Later, he used them in his classical works.

Hungarian pianist and composer Franz Liszt

Zoltán Kodály was especially interested in singing. He developed the famous "Kodály method" of teaching voice and music. This method is still used in Hungarian schools.

An orchestra plays outdoors to a standing-room-only crowd.

A Passion for Words

During the long centuries that their country was under foreign control, Hungarians had to struggle to hold on to their cultural traditions. Perhaps their most treasured tradition was their unique language. Hungarian writers became the spokespeople for the nation. Few people outside of Hungary understood the Hungarian language, however. As a result, for a long time outsiders could not read the works of Hungarian writers. (Many works have now been translated into different languages.)

A great Hungarian poet emerged in the 1600s. Miklós Zrinyi wrote a long patriotic poem called *The Perils of Sziget*. It described the unsuccessful efforts of Hungarians to defend themselves in a battle with the Turks.

In the late 1700s, when the Hapsburgs of Austria ruled Hungary, more patriotic stories came to be written. One was a novel called *Etelka*, by András Dugonics. It was written in response to a decree issued by the Austrian emperor in 1784. The emperor had ruled that German be the official language of the Austrian Empire. Hungarians became alarmed that they would lose their national identity. Language, they knew, was the soul of a nation. As a result, *Etelka* was published. It tells the story of a young girl in the court of Prince Árpád who is forced to speak an unfamiliar language. *Etelka* was meant to give courage to the Hungarian people and help them take pride in their heritage.

Later on, in the 1800s, poems and plays often described the quiet heroism of the people living in the countryside. On stage, folk songs and scenes from farm life were produced. Again, in this way, the Hungarian people could take pride in their national traditions.

Modern Times

After World War I, some writers began to focus on social problems. Attila József wrote about the problems of city life. His poems provide a moving view of the life of the poor.

Perhaps the most famous literary figure of this time was Ferenc Molnár. He wrote plays and novels. Molnár moved to the United States during World War II. There he wrote a number of screenplays for Hollywood movies. One of Molnár's best-known plays was *Liliom*, on which the musical comedy *Carousel* was based.

After World War II, Hungarian literature came under the control of the Communist government. People could not write anything they wanted. But with the fall of communism in

HUNGARIANS IN ARTS AND SCIENCES

Ignaz Semmelweis (1818–1865) was a Hungarian physician. While on the staff of a hospital in Vienna, Semmelweis discovered that infections were spread by unsanitary conditions. He insisted that doctors and nurses involved in childbirth wash their hands. Semmelweis's discoveries led to the introduction of new procedures of cleanliness in the treatment of patients. His ideas were ridiculed at the time, and he returned to Hungary, where he died.

Joseph Pulitzer (1847–1911) was a newspaper publisher. Born in Hungary, he moved to the United States in 1864 and served in the Union Army in the Civil War. Over the course of his career, Pulitzer bought a number of newspapers, including the New York-based *World*. He was a pioneer in the use of illustrations, cartoons, and aggressive news coverage. Pulitzer left money to establish the Pulitzer Prizes, which are awarded each year for excellence in a number of categories, including newspaper reporting and writing.

Bela Lugosi (1884–1956) was a Hollywood actor who was born in Hungary. A classical stage actor in Hungary, Lugosi moved to California in the 1920s and began making movies. His most famous film role was the vampire Count Dracula in the movie of the same name, made in 1931.

Eugene Ormandy (1899–1985) was a world-famous orchestra conductor. He graduated from the Budapest Royal Academy at the age of 14. In 1921, Ormandy moved to the United States. He was appointed conductor of the Minneapolis Symphony in 1931. In 1938, he became the musical director and conductor of the Philadelphia Orchestra. Ormandy made hundreds of recordings with the Philadelphia Orchestra, which listeners continue to enjoy.

Edward Teller (1908–   ) is a physicist. Born in Hungary, Teller became an American citizen in 1941. He taught physics at the University of Chicago and worked at the Los Alamos National Laboratory. There he helped develop the first hydrogen bomb. He later wrote about the peacetime use of nuclear energy.

1989, Hungarian writers were free to express themselves. This new generation of writers, like Hungary's craftspeople, composers, and musicians, can now bring the richness and beauty of Hungary's culture to people all over the world.

Country Facts

Official Name: Magyar Köztársaság (Republic of Hungary)

Capital: Budapest

Location: central Europe. Surrounded by Slovakia and Ukraine on the north; Austria on the west; Slovenia, Serbia, and Croatia on the south; and Romania on the east

Area: 35,920 square miles (93,033 kilometers). *Greatest distances:* east–west, 328 miles (528 kilometers); north–south, 167 miles (269 kilometers)

Elevation: *Highest:* Mount Kékes, in Mátra Mountains, 3,330 feet (1,015 meters). *Lowest:* Tisza River, near Szeged, 256 feet (78 meters)

Climate: temperate—cold winters and hot summers

Population: 10,219,000. *Distribution:* 60 percent urban; 40 percent rural

Form of Government: parliamentary republic

Important Products: *Natural resources:* bauxite; coal; natural gas. *Agriculture:* wheat; corn; barley; rye; oats; potatoes; sugar beets; onions; paprika; grapes; apricots; pears; cherries; apples; plums. *Industries:* iron and steel; machinery; pharmaceuticals; vehicles; communication equipment; milling; distilling

Basic Unit of Money: forint; 1 forint = 100 filler

Languages: Hungarian (Magyar); Gypsy

Religions: Roman Catholic; Calvinist; Lutheran; smaller groups practicing the Eastern Orthodox and Jewish faiths

Flag: three horizontal stripes in red, white, and green

National Anthem: *Isten Áldd Meg a Magyart* ("God Bless the Hungarian")

Major National Holidays: New Year's Day, January 1; Easter Monday (varies yearly); 1848 Revolution Day, March 15; Labor Day, May 1; St. Stephen's Day, August 20; 1956 Uprising Day of Remembrance, October 23; Christmas, December 25 and 26.

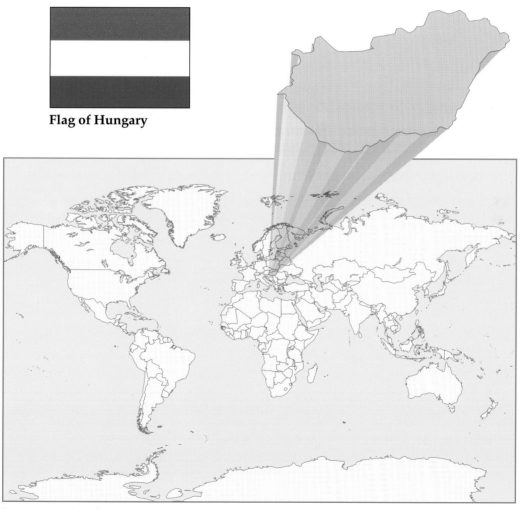

Flag of Hungary

Hungary in the World

Glossary

communism: a form of government in which the state owns and controls all goods and their production

democracy: a political system in which a country is governed by its people and their elected representatives

dual monarchy: a system in which one king rules two lands; in Hungary, the emperor of Austria was also the king of Hungary

goulash (GOO-lahsh)**:** Hungarian stew made of cubes of beef and vegetables, spiced with paprika

Gypsies: the largest ethnic minority in Hungary

Hapsburgs: the Austrian royal family that established control over Hungary in the late 1600s and ruled until the end of the Austrian Empire in 1918

Magyar: Hungarians; the people who settled Hungary about one thousand years ago and from whom most modern Hungarians are descended

paprika: a spice made from a blend of crushed peppers; it is used in much Hungarian cooking

vocational: having to do with work, such as a school that teaches work skills

For Further Reading

Brogan, Patrick. *The Captive Nations: Eastern Europe, 1945-1990*. New York: Avon Books, 1990.

Esbenshade, Richard S. *Hungary*. New York: Marshall Cavendish, 1994.

Lye, Keith. *Take a Trip to Hungary*. New York: Watts, 1986.

Radkai, Marton, Ulrike Segal, and Heinz Vestner. *Hungary*. Boston: Houghton Mifflin, 1995.

Vardy, Steven Bela. *The Hungarian Americans*. New York: Chelsea House, 1990.

Index

Page numbers for illustrations are in boldface

architecture, 27, **28–29**, 53–54
Árpád, Prince, 7–8, 10, 11
arts and crafts, 51–53, **52**
Austria-Hungary, 14, 21
Austrian rule, of Hungary, 11, 12–14
authors, 57–58

Balantonfüred, 46
Balaton, Lake, 8, 46–48, **47**
bathhouses. *See* spas
Battle of Mohács, 11
Budapest, **6**, 27, **30**, 46

cities, 27. *See also* Balantonfüred; Budapest; Debrecen; Györ; Gyula; Hollókö; Miskolc; Nagygálló; Nógrád; Nyiregyháza; Pécs
climate, 8
clothing, **20**, 27, 36, **36**, 52, **53**, 54
communism, 16, 19, 24, 58

Danube River, **6**, 8
Debrecen, 27

family life, **32**, 33–35, **34**
famous Hungarians, 59. *See also* authors; musicians
farming, 24, **25**, 26–27, **26**
folk festivals, 36–37, **37**, 55
food, 38–39, **38**

geography, 8, **9**
government, 18
Great Alföld, 8
Györ, 44
Gypsies, **20**, 21, 22–24, **23**
Gyula, 44

Hapsburg Empire. *See* Austrian rule, of Hungary
history, 9–19
holidays, 35
Hollókö, 54

instruments. *See* music

Kékes, Mount, 8

language, 30–31, 58
Little Alföld, 8

Magyars, 7–8, 10–11, 21
Maria Theresa, Empress, 13, **13**
Mátra Mountains, 8
Matyó, 52

Miskolc, 27, 37, 44, 46
museums, 42–44, **43**
music, 22, **50**, 54–57, **55**, **57**
musicians, 56, **56**

Nagygálló, 37
1956 Revolution, 16–18, **17**
Nógrád, 53
Nyiregyháza, 46

Pannonia, 9–10
Pécs, 27
peoples of, **20**, 21–24, **23**

regions. *See* geography; Matyó; Transdanubia
religion, 24
and holidays, 35

school, **40**, 41–42
Soviet rule, of Hungary, 16–19
spas, 44, **45**, 46
sports and recreation, 42–49, **48**, **49**

Transdanubia, 8
Turkish rule, of Hungary, 11–12, **12**

World War I, 14
World War II, 14–16, **15**, 22
writing, 57–59

About the Author

Richard Steins first visited Europe as a high school student in the early 1960s. He has returned many times since then to pursue his interest in history and the arts.

After receiving a master's degree in history from Columbia University, Richard worked as an editor and writer on a number of encyclopedias. He specialized in history, geography, and literature. He then entered college publishing, serving as the director of development for a textbook publisher.

In 1991, he published his first book for young readers and since then has gone on to publish a number of works in the areas of current events, history, politics, and biography. He is currently writing a book about the American Civil War.